You know you're a <u>real</u> Yooper when...

Written by: Jim Bellmore & Jim DeCaire

Illustrations by: Jim Bellmore

Library of Congress Card No. 97-090631
ISBN 0-9658645-0-2
First Edition-1997
Revised Edition-1997

Published by You Guys Inc.
Ishpeming, Michigan 49849

Printed in Michigan, U.S.A. by
Lake Superior Press
Marquette, Michigan 49855

Backward...

This book is meant to be humorous. You Guys Inc. will not be held responsible for any misuse or misinterpretation of its contents. In other words, laugh and have fun, the world is too serious as it is.

Any similarities to fictional caricatures are pretty coincidental cause we wouldn't want to embarrass those whom resemble said fictional characters which are within these pages.

You know you're a real Yooper when…

…Your best man at your wedding drinks both kegs of beer before the first dance.

...You get married and half of the people at your reception are strangers that come for the free beer.

...Your favorite kind of beer is free beer.

You know you're a <u>real</u> Yooper when...

...You have to ski out your upstairs bedroom window to get to work.

…Your dad starts his father-son talk with, "When I was your age I had to walk ten miles through six foot snow drifts to get to school."

…You have at least seven pairs of skis out gathering dust in your garage or basement.

You know you're a real Yooper when...

...You pretend to be sleeping in hopes the wife will get up and blow out the four foot snow drifts in the driveway.

…January comes along and you wish someone would come and run over Heikki Lunta *(the snow God of the U.P.)* accidentally on purpose.

…You're the envy of all the buddies cause your wife let you buy a V-10, 4X4 pickup with a really big plow.

You know you're a <u>real</u> Yooper when...

...Your long johns are part of your daily attire, all year around.

...You go swimming in July and draw straws to see who will jump in the lake first to break the ice.

...You survive the torturous, 2 week, 80 degree hot spell the U.P. gets once a decade.

You know you're a <u>real</u> Yooper when...

...You have a rummage sale just to get rid of your unused collection of exercise machines.

...You consider a luxury car anything built before 1985 with a good heater and no rust.

...You sit around on a hot summer night listening to your new car rust.

You know you're a real Yooper when...

...Your dad was dressing "grunge" decades before "grunge" was cool.

...Your dad starts every argument with, "When I was your age I had to chop and pile wood everyday after school."

...You ask your dad to borrow the new family car to impress your date and he proudly lets you use his 72 Nova rust bucket piece of junk.

You know you're a <u>real</u> Yooper when...

...Your mother tells you the way to catch a husband is to learn how to run and maintain a snowblower.

…Your mother keeps her snowblower tuned up and ready all year around.

…You're 24 and living at home and your mother still enforces a 10:00 p.m. curfew.

You know you're a <u>real</u> Yooper when...

...You use an outhouse at least once a month.

…You've taken more saunas than showers.

…Your buddies measure distance traveled by how many beers were drank from point A to point B.

You know you're a <u>real</u> Yooper when...

...You're getting the worst snow storm of the century and your mother-in-law who's never driven demands, "It ain't bad out there, take me to Shopko!"

….Your weekly check is $3.00 less than what you've spent on salt for the driveway.

….Your mother-in-law moves in with you and your beer bill goes up to $100.00 a week.

You know you're a <u>real</u> Yooper when...

...You throw a party and wind up serving drinks in Packer mugs and Little Mermaid glasses.

…You sign a petition to have Vincent Lombardi canonized St. Vincent Lombardi—guardian of the Packers.

…You consider Green Bay the capital of Yooperland and Wisconsin the banana belt.

You know you're a real Yooper when...

...Your movie rental bill is your largest bill in the winter.

...You have a masters degree in business and end up managing a movie rental shop in the U.P.

...You have to take a dog sleigh to the nearest trading post to rent a movie.

You know you're a <u>real</u> Yooper when...

...The conversation turns to world affairs and the only topics that come to mind are snow and the Packers.

...It's more important to watch Buck Le Vasseur than the Presidential debate.

...You place bets with your buddies on whose car is going to rust first.

You know you're a <u>real</u> Yooper when…

…You can detect a Yooper-wanna-be from Detroit by their fake Yooper accents.

…You know that Traverse City, Cadillac, Houghton Lake and Grayling are in *central* Michigan, not *northern* Michigan like they claim.

…You go down-state and find a Michigan map t-shirt with the U.P. missing and you really don't care.

You know you're a <u>real</u> Yooper when...

...Your snowmobile gets more tune-ups than the family car.

...Your survival gear in your truck consists of jumper cables, snow shovel, sand bags, toilet paper, winch, duct tape and a baseball bat for killing mosquitoes while making bush calls.

...Your wife has to park her car outside because the garage is all filled up with empty returnable cans.

You know you're a real Yooper when...

...You think the only true breed of dog is beagle and all others are mutts.

…Your answering machine says, "I'm not here. I may be out duck hunting, deer hunting, bird hunting, rabbit hunting, or fishing so don't leave a message."

…You consider "deer" one of the five seasons of the year: *spring, summer, fall, deer, and winter.*

You know you're a <u>real</u> Yooper when...

...You ask your mother for new clothes and she says, "When I was your age I had two dresses, one for Sunday, and the other for everyday."

…You ask your mother for new shoes and she answers, "When I was your age, I had one pair of shoes and when they wore out, I'd put cardboard in them."

…You work your butt off to get good grades so you can attend Michigan Tech, cause the ratio is 100 guys to 1 woman.

You know you're a <u>real</u> Yooper when...

...You believe the Native Americans are taking back the U.P. a quarter at a time.

…Your wife donates part of your paycheck to the local Native American Indian Reservation at least once a month.

…A police officer in Green Bay gives you a ticket for J-walking and he has to explain what J-walking is.

You know you're a real Yooper when...

...It's deer season and you go Shopko to buy a new "bag a single buck" outfit consisting of army fatigue pants, plaid shirt, down vest, and a ball cap.

...You dine once a week on any of these Yooper soul foods: *cudighi, morel mushrooms, smelt, pasty, blueberry pie, venison, partridge, smoked lake trout, baked whitefish, Trenary toast, limpo, fillia, and moyika.*

...You consider plaid the Yooperland national color and partridge the national bird.

You know you're a <u>real</u> Yooper when...

...You've lived in a neighborhood where at least one kid and a dog were carried off by mosquitoes.

...You have had all of the following insects bite you at the same time: mosquito, noseeum, sand fly, horsefly, fish fly, wood tick, and deer fly.

...The drone from mosquitoes is louder than your husband's snoring.

You know you're a <u>real</u> Yooper when...

...Your wife gives you your allowance the same day as the kids.

...You ask your dad for money and he always says the same thing, "Go ask your mother, like I do."

...You take the wife to Green Bay shopping for the weekend and you bring your own beer to drink in the room, cause you ain't paying $3.00 a bottle down at the bar.

You know you're a real Yooper when...

...Your family wants to go to Disney Land every year, but you can never afford it because you're broke from your yearly vacation at deer camp.

…You've been going to deer camp for 27 years and the only shots you've fired are down your throat.

…You spend more time playing cards at deer camp than hunting.

You know you're a real Yooper when...

...Your snowmobile has more duct tape on it than the hardware store.

...You own most of the following: camp, snowblower, chain saw, 4-wheel drive truck, RTV, snow scoop, snowshoes, skis, snow shovel, toboggan, and sleigh.

...Your downstate buddies with their big sleds consider your Yooper snow rocket the safest snow machine on the trail, cause it can only go 30 miles per hour.

You know you're a <u>real</u> Yooper when…

…You vacation down south in the Winter and the people all think you're crazy because you're wearing shorts and a t-shirt.